Tales of Tricks

Plays from Around the World

*Written by Katie Dennison
and Jane Langford*

Contents

How to Read the Plays

There are three plays in this book for you to read aloud in a small group. There are six characters in each play.

1   Choose a character.

2   Look through the play at your character's lines.

3   Read your lines quietly to yourself.

4   Read the whole play aloud in your group.

Reading tips

- Follow the play carefully, even when it is not your turn to read.

- Read your lines clearly.

- Try to speak in the way your character would. If you think your character is loud and bossy, then read your part in a loud, bossy voice.

The Spider's Tricks

A Play by Jane Langford

Illustrations by Michael Terry

Cast

Sky God

Anansi
(the trickster
spider)

Aso
(Anansi's wife)

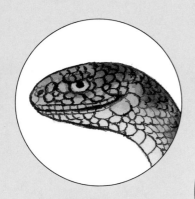

Python

Hornet

Leopard

The Spider's Tricks

Act 1
At the Sky God's palace

Aso Go on then! Go in! Ask the Sky God if you can have the stories.

Anansi I'm going! I'm going! Don't rush me!

Aso Rush you? You're supposed to be a *brave* and *clever* spider, so go on! *(Pushes Anansi through curtained doorway)*

Sky God   Anansi – the trickster spider!
              What brings you to my palace?

Anansi   Well … I have heard that you have got
              a collection of stories, beautiful stories.
              Stories that can be told a thousand
              times without losing any of their beauty.
              And I wondered if I could have them for
              the children on earth.

Aso   Human children *need* stories.

Sky God   We all need stories.

Anansi   But you've got them *all* and it doesn't
              seem fair.

Sky God   Don't talk to me of fairness! I am the
              Sky God. I own the stories. Why should
              I give them to you?

Anansi   Because I asked. Because you're good
              and kind and just and generous and …

Sky God   Stop, stop, stop! No more flattery!
You can have my stories, Anansi.
BUT first you have to give me
something in return.

Anansi   What can I give you? I'm only a spider.

Sky God   Yes, but a cunning and clever one, with
enough brains to trick a dozen men.

Anansi   Who's trying flattery now?

Sky God   It's not flattery, Anansi. It's the truth.
You're very clever and you can perform
a great service for me and all the
animals of the jungle.

Anansi   All right. It's a deal. Now, what do
I have to do?

Sky God   Simple! You merely have to catch the
three most hated creatures in the
jungle: the python with the strongest
squeeze, the hornet with the sharpest
sting, and the leopard with the
cruellest claws.

Aso   But they've ruled the jungle with terror
for year upon year!

Sky God   That's why I need you to catch them for
me. Let me show you where they are.
(Parts clouds and looks down to earth)
There – talking together in that
jungle clearing.

Python   What a wonderful day for squeezing the life out of little creatures! It's such fun!

Hornet   Squeezing is not as much fun as stinging. It's such perfect bliss to terrify other animals that I never want to stop!

Leopard   Stinging and squeezing are nothing compared to scratching and biting soft, furry creatures. It's what I do best!

Aso   *(Looking down at jungle clearing)*
That's terrible! How cruel they are.

Sky God   Yes. That is why I want you to capture
them. Can you do it, Anansi?

Aso   Of course he can.

Anansi   I'm not sure. But I'll try.

Act 2

Later that day, in the jungle clearing

Leopard Why do Anansi and Aso keep staring at us?

Python I don't know, but I am going to find out. Hey! Anansi! Anansi! What are you doing?

Anansi Er – nothing much. I've just been to visit the Sky God.

Leopard A humble little spider like you – visit the Sky God. No, you haven't!

Sky God   *(Peeping through clouds)* Yes, he has.
He has made a request for my
collection of stories.

Hornet   Oh, has he! I could tell him a good
story – with a sharp sting in the tail!

Python   I could tell him one that would squeeze
the breath out of him!

Leopard   I could tell him one that would leave its
mark on him!

Sky God   You can sting, squeeze and scratch all you like, but you won't stop Anansi. He's going to trap the three of you and put an end to the misery you cause in the jungle.

Hornet   Catch us? Ha! Don't be ridiculous!

Leopard   He's only a spider!

Python   He certainly couldn't catch me, not even with that sticky little web of his.

Anansi   Are you sure about that?

Python   Positive!

Anansi   Then let me try.

Leopard *(Laughing loudly)* Go on, Python!
Let him try!

Aso Yes, let him try.

Python I'll let you try. But if you fail, my curling
coils will squeeze the life out of you.
Is that a deal?

Anansi Yes – it's a deal. Lie down over there,
please – on the branch of that tree.

Python slithers over to the branch, grinning widely.

Python Is this the right place?

Anansi Yes, perfect. Now just stay still.

Anansi begins to spin a silken thread. He wraps it round and round Python's tail.

Python   Have you finished yet?

Anansi   No, not quite.

Python   Well hurry up. My coils are getting restless. They feel the need to *squeeeeeze* something!

Aso   Go to sleep then. It won't take long.

Python   *(Yawns)* I am a little tired. I'll take a nap for five minutes … then I'm going to crush you in my coils!

Python falls asleep and Anansi pulls down creepers from the tree. Together with Aso, he wraps them round Python's head and tail. Python is stuck fast. Leopard suddenly notices what has been happening.

Leopard   Python! Wake up! Wake up!
You're stuck!

Python   *(Yawns)* No, I'm not!

Hornet   Yes, you are!

Python   *(Struggles to get free)* I am stuck! I am! I've been tricked! Help! Let me go!

Sky God   I'm afraid not! You've squeezed your last squeeze! You'll stay where you are until you learn how to control those cruel coils of yours.

Python   Leopard! Hornet! Help me!

Leopard   Sorry, old chap! You got yourself into that fix! I'm going!

Hornet   That goes for me too, old boy. That spider's not going to trick me!

Leopard and Hornet leave.

Act 3
Later that day, deep in the jungle

Anansi Right! Are you ready?

Aso I certainly am, Anansi. My feet are ready to start tapping on this leaf. Tap, tap, tap! It will sound just like the patter of raindrops.

Anansi And when Hornet hears rain, he will want to hide. And where will he want to hide? In this calabash, of course!

Sky God *(Peeping through clouds)* But how do you know that Hornet will fly this way?

Anansi He always flies along this path to his nest. He will come, sooner or later.

Hornet Bzzz, bzzz, bzzz.

Anansi Sooner, I think. He's coming now!

Hornet Who would have thought that Anansi could be so sharp-witted and cunning? Next time I see him, I shall sting him all over. That'll teach him which one of us is sharp!

Aso Tap, tap, tap!
Tap, tap, tap!

Hornet Oh no! It's starting to rain. I can't risk getting wet or I won't be able to fly! Now, where can I hide until the shower is over?

Aso Move out of the way! I can't bear getting wet. *(Slides down to the calabash on a thread)* I'm going to hide in this calabash!

Hornet No, you're not! I saw it first! Get out of my way! *(Zooms past Aso and dives straight into calabash)*

Anansi *(Puts lid on calabash)* GOT YOU! You won't be able to sting anybody now.

Hornet Anansi? Is that you? Let me out of here!

Sky God I'm afraid not. You've stung your last sting. You'll stay in that calabash until you learn how to control your sting!

Anansi That will take a long time! … Right, there's just one cruel creature left to catch and then the stories are mine!

Sky God Well hurry, Anansi. It's starting to get dark.

Anansi Doesn't Leopard always hunt in the dark?

Aso Yes, his eyes shine like torches.

Anansi Good. My plan will work better in the dark. Aso, come with me.

Aso and Anansi go down towards the river. Near to the river is a waterhole that has recently dried up.

Anansi He won't cause any more trouble once he's in that hole.

Sky God   *(Peeping through clouds again)* Surely you don't think he's so easily tricked? He won't fall in that hole!

Anansi   You haven't heard my plan yet. We're going to cover up the hole. First, we will spin an enormous web over the hole.

Aso   Then we will climb up into the overhanging tree and … tap, tap, tap … we'll tap the branches and shake the leaves all over the trap!

Anansi and Aso start to prepare the trap. They spin the web, then cover it with leaves.

Aso   Now what are we going to do?

Anansi   Watch and wait! Leopard always hunts by the river.

Anansi runs into the centre of the trap to wait for Leopard. Leopard appears from behind a bush.

Leopard   That's right, Anansi. I am hunting as always, but this time I'm hunting for *you*! (Charges at Anansi and falls straight into pit)

Leopard   Aaargh! Let me out! Let me out!

Sky God   I'm afraid not. You've scratched your last scratch. You will stay in that pit until you learn to keep your scratches to yourself!

Anansi   You can't keep the stories to yourself any longer, Sky God. They are mine now!

Sky God   They certainly are, Anansi! From now on they shall be known as Anansi's Stories and you can tell them to children all over the world!

Birbal's Trick

A Play by Katie Dennison

Illustrations by Diana Mayo

Cast

Narrator

Akbar,
the Emperor of
India

Vikra,
a nobleman

Birbal,
a poor man

Tansen,
a rich musician

The King of
Burma

Birbal's Trick

Act 1

Narrator *Many years ago, a famous emperor called Akbar ruled over India. One day, a quarrel arose between Akbar and Vikra, one of his noblemen.*

Akbar I have decided that Birbal is going to be my chief advisor.

Vikra *(Very shocked)* Birbal! My Lord, why do you want Birbal to be your advisor? He isn't of noble birth. He isn't even rich. In fact, he's very poor.

Akbar   I have chosen him because I want a clever advisor, and Birbal is the cleverest man I know.

Vikra   Well, what about Tansen, your musician? He's very talented and he comes from a rich and noble family. He would be far better than Birbal.

Akbar   I need someone who is clever and wise. Tansen is a great musician, but he is not as wise as Birbal.

Narrator   *Akbar knew that if Vikra disagreed with him, then the other noblemen would as well. So he decided to call a meeting. Birbal and Tansen were both invited.*

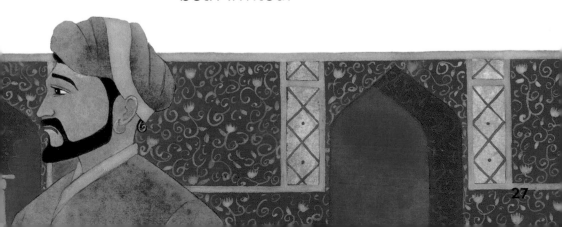

Akbar My noblemen, I have asked you here today because I know you are unhappy about my choice of chief advisor.

Vikra We all think that Birbal is too poor and humble to be a chief advisor to the Emperor of India.

Akbar I understand that you would like me to choose Tansen.

Vikra Everyone agrees that Tansen would be the best choice, my Lord.

Akbar I cannot rule well if my people think my decisions are wrong. I must prove to you that my decision is right.

Vikra How will you do that, my Lord?

Akbar I am going to set the two men a challenge. Whoever wins will prove himself to be the cleverest. This man will be my chief advisor. Does everyone agree?

Narrator *Vikra whispered with the other noblemen for a few moments.*

Vikra Yes, we all agree. Whoever wins the challenge will have proved himself to be the wiser man and should be your chief advisor.

Tansen *(Nervously)* What challenge have you set us, my Lord?

Akbar I am condemning you both to die. Whoever can save himself will become my advisor.

Narrator *A shocked silence greeted Akbar's words, until at last Birbal spoke.*

Birbal But how will you condemn us to death, my Lord?

Akbar I have here a letter to my brother, the King of Burma. The letter asks him to put you both to death. Vikra, my trusted noble, will take you both to Burma and give this letter to my brother.

Vikra Your brother is bound to do as you ask.

Tansen Whatever can we do? The King of Burma will kill us both!

Akbar That is your challenge. Whoever can save his own life and return here shall be my advisor.

Act 2

Narrator   *So Vikra took Birbal and Tansen to Burma. The journey took many days, but finally they arrived and asked to meet the King.*

King of Burma   Welcome, Vikra. Do you come with a message from my brother, Akbar?

Vikra   Yes, your Highness.

King of Burma   Who are these two men you bring in chains to my country?

Vikra   These two men are Tansen and Birbal. I have brought a letter from the Emperor about them.

Narrator   *The King took the letter from Vikra and read it.*

King of Burma   I don't understand. Why is my brother asking me to kill these men? Is there something else I should know?

Vikra   No, your Highness.

King of Burma   Have you both committed such terrible crimes that the Emperor does not want your bones or ashes on his land?

Birbal   We have done no wrong, your Highness.

King of Burma   You must have done something!
Unless you tell me, you will be
killed, just as Akbar asks. Guards,
take these men away. Lock them
up in the deepest prison cell. Their
execution will take place a week
from today.

Narrator   *So Tansen and Birbal were locked
in a small, dark cell.*

Tansen   Listen, Birbal – this isn't my fault.
I am a musician and I don't even
want to be Akbar's advisor. What
can we do to make the King of
Burma change his mind?

Birbal   I don't know yet, but we must think
up some kind of plan.

Narrator *A week later, Tansen and Birbal were brought before the King. Outside, in the courtyard, a large area had been cleared, ready for Birbal and Tansen to be killed.*

Birbal *(Loudly)* I must die first!

Tansen *(Angrily)* I am the most important, I must die before you!

Birbal *(Shouting)* I tell you, I must be killed first!

King of Burma What is going on? Why are you arguing about who should die first? This is very strange.

Birbal   Your Highness, Akbar had a special reason for wanting us to die, but we can't tell you.

King of Burma   Vikra, is this true? Why can't these men tell me? Why does my brother want these men killed?

Vikra   I promised Akbar that I would not tell you, your Highness.

King of Burma   Come here, you two. I must know what you have done. If you don't tell me, then I shall have to carry out my brother's orders.

Act 3

Narrator *Birbal and Tansen knelt before the King of Burma.*

Birbal *(Nervously)* I see that I shall have to tell you why Akbar wants you to kill us. Even though he is Emperor of all India, he wants even more land. He asked his wise men how he could take over Burma as well.

King of Burma *(Shocked and upset)* My brother wants my land! How could he do this to me? What did the wise men say he should do to get my land?

Birbal They told Akbar to send two innocent men to you and ask that you put them to death.

Tansen We are the two men Akbar chose, your Highness.

King of Burma But how is that going to allow him to take my land?

Birbal The wise men told Akbar that if you killed two innocent men, they would be reborn and live again and *you* would die. In their new lives, one of the men would become the King of Burma and the other, the King's chief advisor.

Tansen We are loyal servants of the Emperor. He knew that if one of us became the King of Burma, we would give the land to him.

King of Burma You mean my brother tried to trick me into killing you so that he could take my land?

Birbal Yes, your Highness.

Tansen *(Whispering to Vikra)* But really Birbal's plan is to trick the King and to save our lives!

Vikra *(Whispering to Tansen)* I wondered what Birbal was up to.

King of Burma I tell you, my brother will never take this land from me. I am King of Burma and I intend to rule this land for many years to come. Vikra, you can take that message back to my brother.

Vikra I will, your Highness.

King of Burma But I still don't understand why you were arguing about who should die first.

Birbal That's easy to explain. The man who died first would become the King of Burma and we both want to be the King!

King of Burma You shall not die on my land. Now return to your Emperor and tell him I know about his plans.

Vikra We shall return immediately.

King of Burma *(Angrily)* And tell my brother that I know about his greedy ways. He shall never take Burma from me!

Narrator *So Birbal and Tansen escaped death and returned to India with Vikra. When Akbar learned how Birbal had tricked the King of Burma, he sent for his noblemen.*

Akbar   Let me tell you how Birbal and Tansen escaped death. When you hear it, I know you will agree that Birbal is clever enough to be a great advisor for our country.

Narrator   *The nobles listened in amazement to the story of how Birbal tricked the King of Burma and saved his life and Tansen's. The nobles talked amongst themselves for a few minutes. At last Vikra spoke.*

Vikra My Lord, your decision was right. Birbal may be a poor man but he is certainly clever. We all agree that he should become your chief advisor.

Akbar Thank you, Vikra. Now Tansen, will you continue to be my musician?

Tansen It is all I have ever wanted to be, my Lord.

Akbar Good. Now, Birbal, I have a job for you. You must write a letter to my brother immediately. Tell him about the challenge I set you and make it clear I do not want his land. The job of a good advisor is to ensure peace and friendship between countries.

Birbal *(Smiling)* It will be a pleasure, my Lord.

Narrator So that is how Birbal saved his own
life and tricked the King of Burma.
Many stories have been told about
Birbal and how his cleverness helped
the Emperor, Akbar.

Kahu's Trick

A Play by Katie Dennison

Illustrations by Martin Ursell

Cast

Narrator

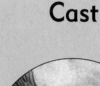

Chief Waikato
(Why-ca-to)

Kahu – his son
(Car-hoo)

Chief Whenua
(Fen-oo-a)

Koka – his daughter
(Co-ca)

Taniwha – a
mighty dragon
(Tun-ee-far)

Kahu's Trick

Act 1

Narrator *Long, long ago, when people and animals could talk together, a taniwha lived high up on a mountain. In the valleys on either side of this mountain, there lived two tribes.*

Chief Waikato Listen, my son, it is time you were married. You must go to visit Chief Whenua and ask his daughter to be your wife.

Kahu I will gladly go to see the old chief, for I have heard that his daughter is both beautiful and clever.

Chief Waikato   You must take the path around the mountain – don't go over the top. The great old taniwha lives there, and he eats anyone who passes his cave.

Kahu   But the path over the top would be much quicker, Father.

Chief Waikato   It is far too dangerous to go over the mountain. You must go around it.

Kahu   But Father, you have killed so many taniwhas, why are you so scared of this one?

Chief Waikato None of the taniwhas that I killed were as cunning or dangerous as this one. And his skin has become so tough with age that no sword or arrow can pierce it.

Kahu One day, I will find a way of getting rid of the taniwha. But for now, I will go around the mountain as you say.

Narrator *So Kahu set off around the mountain. He walked for two days until he came to the home of Koka and her father, Chief Whenua.*

Chief Whenua   Greetings, Kahu. What brings you to this side of the mountain?

Kahu   I have come to ask your daughter to marry me.

Chief Whenua   It is time my daughter was wed and I would gladly have her married to the son of my old friend, Chief Waikato. Koka, what do you say?

Narrator *Koka smiled at Kahu shyly and nodded.*

Chief Whenua There is one thing though, Kahu. I am an old man and I want to see my daughter often. Therefore, I cannot have her living two days' journey from me. If you want to marry her, you must get rid of the taniwha first.

Kahu *(Bravely)* Then I shall go back over the mountain now and challenge the taniwha.

Koka Be very careful, Kahu. Many of our tribe have tried to cross the mountain but none have come back.

Chief Whenua Your father was a great slayer of taniwhas. Doesn't he know how to get rid of him?

Kahu My father has told me that no sword or arrow can pierce his skin, so I must think of a way to trick him into leaving the mountain.

Koka I have heard that when taniwhas are very old, their scales itch so much that they will do anything to have their backs scratched. I have also heard that their favourite meal of all is young girls!

Kahu Thank you, Koka. I will remember what you have told me.

Koka I shall wait for you to return. In the meantime, I will prepare the wedding feast.

Act 2

Narrator *So Kahu set off along the narrow path that led over the mountain. As he climbed, he thought about what Koka had told him.*

Taniwha *(Loudly)* Who is that daring to cross my mountain?

Kahu It is I, Son of Chief Waikato. I have come to talk to you.

Taniwha Ha! I have a much better plan and it does not involve talking.

Kahu Listen to me. Let me come in and I will scratch your back. Then I will tell you what I can do for you.

Taniwha Very well. Anyone who enters my cave is unlikely to leave it except in my stomach. But before I eat you, you may scratch my back.

Narrator   *Kahu walked into the gloomy cave and began to scratch the taniwha's back.*

Kahu   I know you want to eat me, but I can get you a young girl who will taste far better than I do. She will scratch your back and then you can eat her. Think how delicious that would be. But in return you must promise to do something for me.

Taniwha   A young girl is a meal worth waiting for, but what must I promise?

Kahu   You must promise to leave this mountain and live far away. I want to marry Koka and her father wants a safe path over the mountain so that he can visit us.

Taniwha   All right. Bring me a girl and put her on my back. Then I will fly away and you will never see me again.

Narrator   *So Kahu went back to his tribe and told his father what had happened.*

Chief Waikato   *(Shocked)* What have you done? You cannot give a girl to that monster!

Kahu   I never said the girl would be real! I shall make her out of straw. That way she will scratch the taniwha's back nicely, and in the gloom of his cave he will not see her. He will fly far away before he realises that he has been tricked.

Narrator *So the people of Kahu's tribe all helped him make a straw girl. When she was ready, Kahu set off again up the mountain.*

Kahu O Taniwha, I have brought you a beautiful girl to scratch your back.

Taniwha Bring her into my cave and put her on my back.

Narrator *Kahu went into the cave and carefully put the straw girl onto the taniwha's back.*

Kahu   Don't forget you said you would
leave the mountain!

Taniwha   I shall fly far from here and then she
will scratch my back for me. Why, I
can feel her scratching me already.

Narrator   *Then Kahu ran down the mountain
to Koka.*

Koka   The feast is all ready, Kahu. Have
you got rid of the taniwha?

Kahu   Yes, he has flown far away and will
not return. Now we can be wed.

Act 3

Narrator   *The feasting lasted for many days. Then Kahu and Koka and all the people made their way over the mountain to Kahu's village. As they went, they cut down trees and began to make a good wide path.*

Koka   While you are helping the people make the path, I will go ahead and prepare a feast for when you have finished.

Narrator   *But unknown to Kahu and the people, the taniwha had returned to the mountain. He was angry about Kahu's trick.*

Taniwha *(Fiercely)* I hear the sound of footsteps. I shall soon have a tasty meal.

Narrator *When Koka neared the entrance of the cave, the taniwha sprang on her and carried her to the back of the cave.*

Koka *(Terrified)* Help! Help!

Taniwha There is no help for you. You cannot escape and no one can harm me. Wait until Kahu comes along and I tell him about this prize.

Narrator   *When Kahu heard what had happened, he was very upset. He knew he must kill the taniwha, but how?*

Chief Whenua   You must rescue my daughter. Unless this beast is killed, we will never be safe.

Narrator   *Kahu sat alone for many hours, thinking and thinking. Finally, he returned to the people and asked that a huge rope be made. Then one hundred men followed Kahu to the taniwha's cave.*

Kahu Take this rope and hide in the rocks above the cave. Hang the noose down in front of the entrance. I will get the taniwha to come out, and when he does, pull on the rope as hard as you can.

Narrator *Then Kahu went up to the cave of the taniwha. He stood outside and began to speak.*

Kahu Listen, Scabby Scales! I hear that you have got Koka. She won't make a good meal. She is too thin and bony.

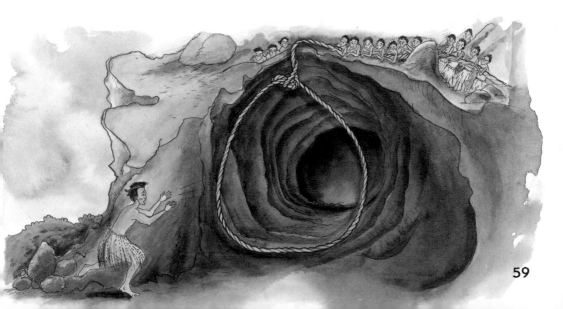

Taniwha She will do for now and I shall get you later.

Kahu What! You are too old and stupid to catch me *now*?

Taniwha I am the greatest taniwha that has ever lived. No one is as powerful as I am.

Koka Save yourself and the people, Kahu. Don't come any nearer or he will eat you as well.

Kahu Why, you are old and useless, Taniwha! Look, I am standing just outside your cave, but I can still escape from you.

Taniwha No one can escape from me. I will get you and squeeze you to death, Kahu. You have no magic powers against me. I am the greatest taniwha that has ever lived.

Narrator *Then the taniwha rushed out of the cave and the noose slipped over his head. The men pulled and pulled, and as the noose tightened it choked the taniwha to death.*

Koka   You have saved us all, Kahu. Now we will never be afraid to cross the mountain again.

Chief Waikato   Indeed, my son, you have rid us of this horrible beast.

Chief Whenua   And you shall be called ... Kahu, the mighty.

Narrator   *So that is how Kahu, the mighty, tricked the great taniwha.*